Pebble® Plus
Healthy Teeth

At the Dentist

by Mari Schuh

Consulting Editor:
Gail Saunders-Smith, PhD

Consultant:
Lori Gagliardi CDA, RDA, RDH, EdD

Capstone
press
Mankato, Minnesota

Pebble Plus is published by Capstone Press,
151 Good Counsel Drive, P.O. Box 669, Mankato, Minnesota 56002.
www.capstonepress.com

1 2 3 4 5 6 13 12 11 10 09 08

Library of Congress Cataloging-in-Publication Data
Schuh, Mari C., 1975–
    At the dentist/by Mari Schuh.
    p. cm. — (Pebble plus. Healthy teeth)
    Summary: "Simple text, photographs, and diagrams present information about going to the dentist and
how to take care of teeth properly"— Provided by publisher.
    Includes bibliographical references and index.
    ISBN-13: 978-1-4296-1242-5 (hardcover)
    ISBN-10: 1-4296-1242-8 (hardcover)
    ISBN-13: 978-1-4296-1788-8 (softcover)
    ISBN-10: 1-4296-1788-8 (softcover)
    1. Dentistry — Juvenile literature. 2. Teeth — Care and hygiene — Juvenile literature.
3. Children — Preparation for dental care — Juvenile literature. I. Title. II. Series.
RK63.S36 2008
617.6 — dc22   2007027119

Editorial Credits
Sarah L. Schuette, editor; Veronica Bianchini, designer

Photo Credits
Capstone Press/Karon Dubke, all

The author dedicates this book to her childhood dentist, Dr. Fred Carlson of Fairmont, Minnesota.

Note to Parents and Teachers

The Healthy Teeth set supports national science standards related to personal health.
This book describes and illustrates going to the dentist. The images support early readers
in understanding the text. The repetition of words and phrases helps early readers learn
new words. This book also introduces early readers to subject-specific vocabulary words,
which are defined in the Glossary section. Early readers may need assistance to read
some words and to use the Table of Contents, Glossary, Read More, Internet Sites, and
Index sections of the book.

Table of Contents

Teeth Checkups

Lena visits the dentist's office twice a year.

Her teeth need a checkup.

Dentist Doug greets Lena.
He shows her where
to sit for her exam.

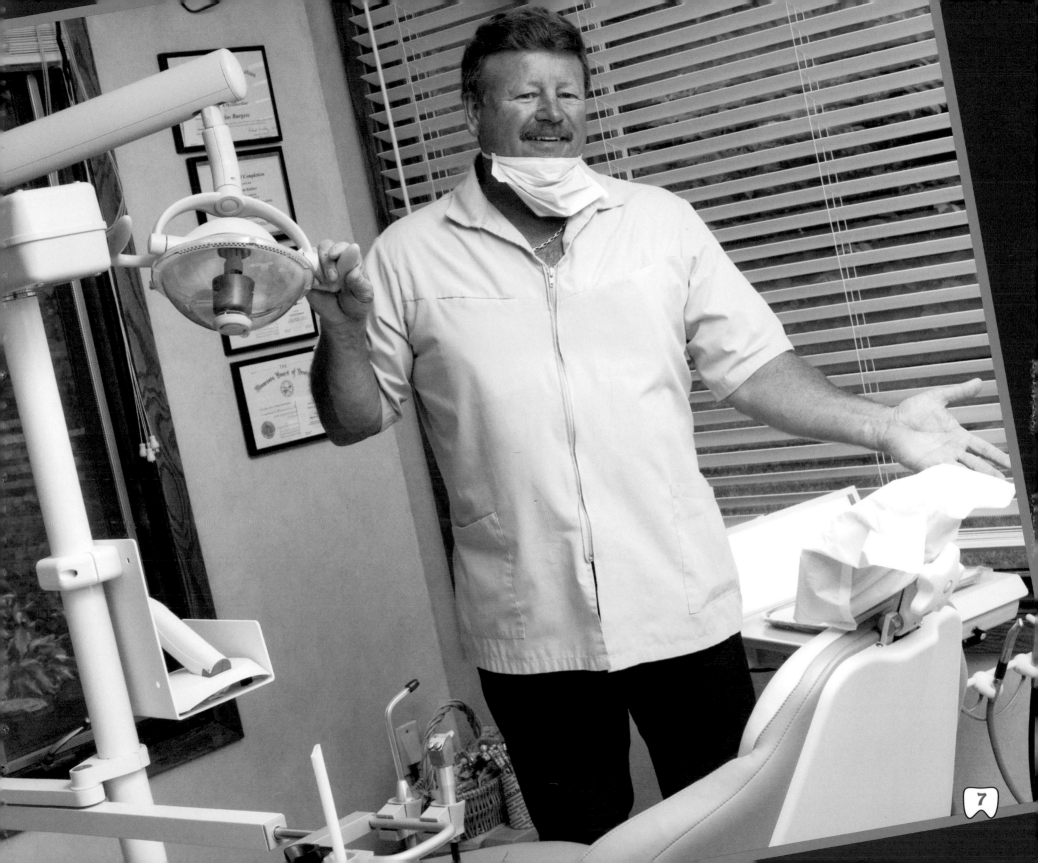

What Happens

Deb the hygienist teaches
Lena about her teeth.
Lena learns how
to brush and floss.

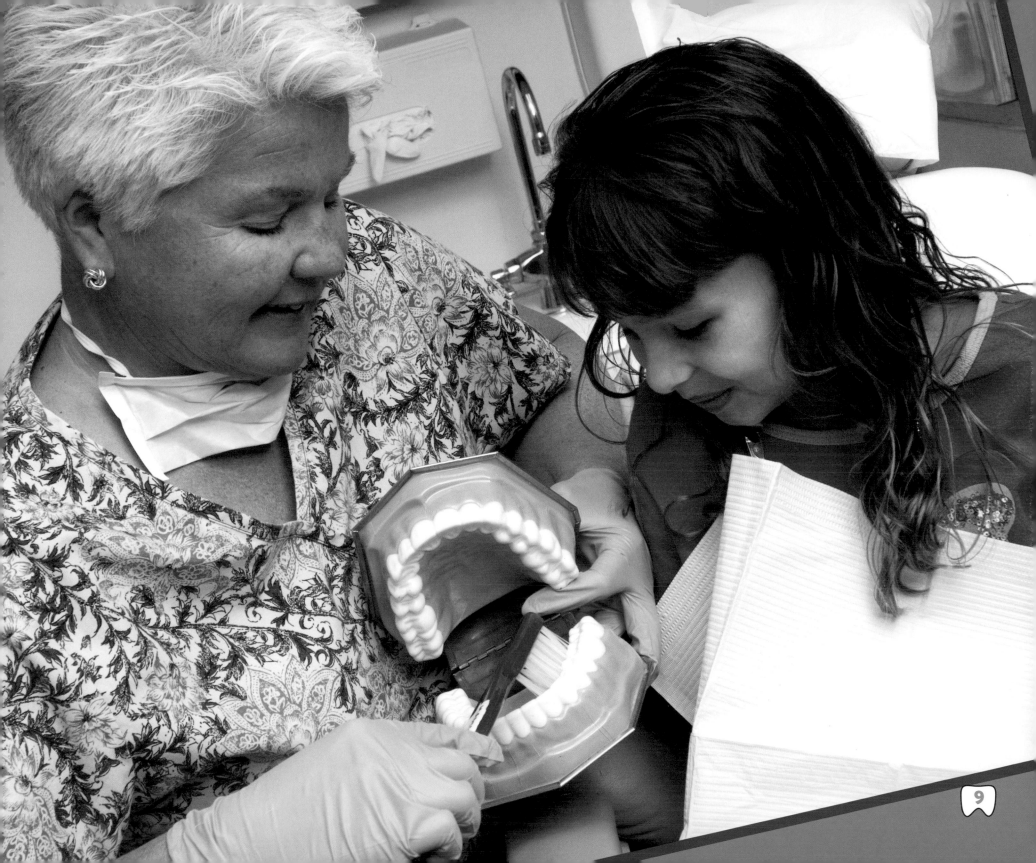

Lena has x-rays taken.
X-rays are pictures
of her teeth and gums.

11

Deb cleans the plaque
from Lena's teeth.
Deb polishes and flosses
Lena's teeth too.

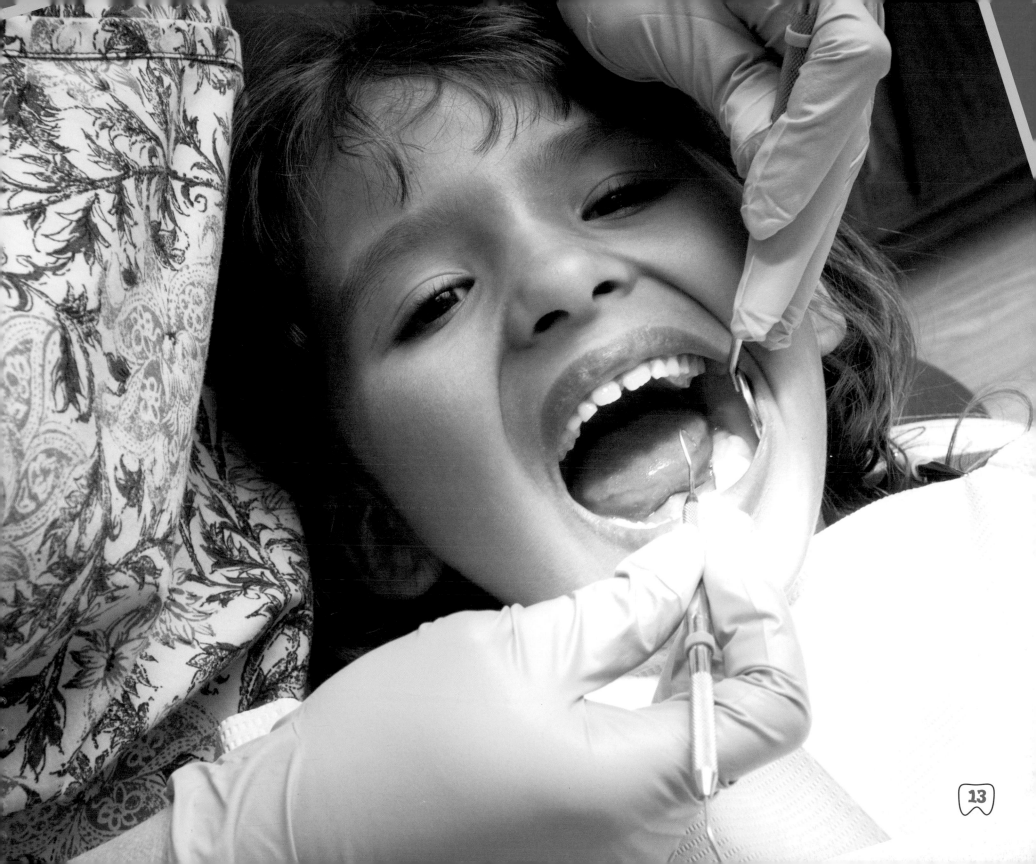

Cavities

Then Deb puts sealants on Lena's teeth. Sealants protect teeth from cavities.

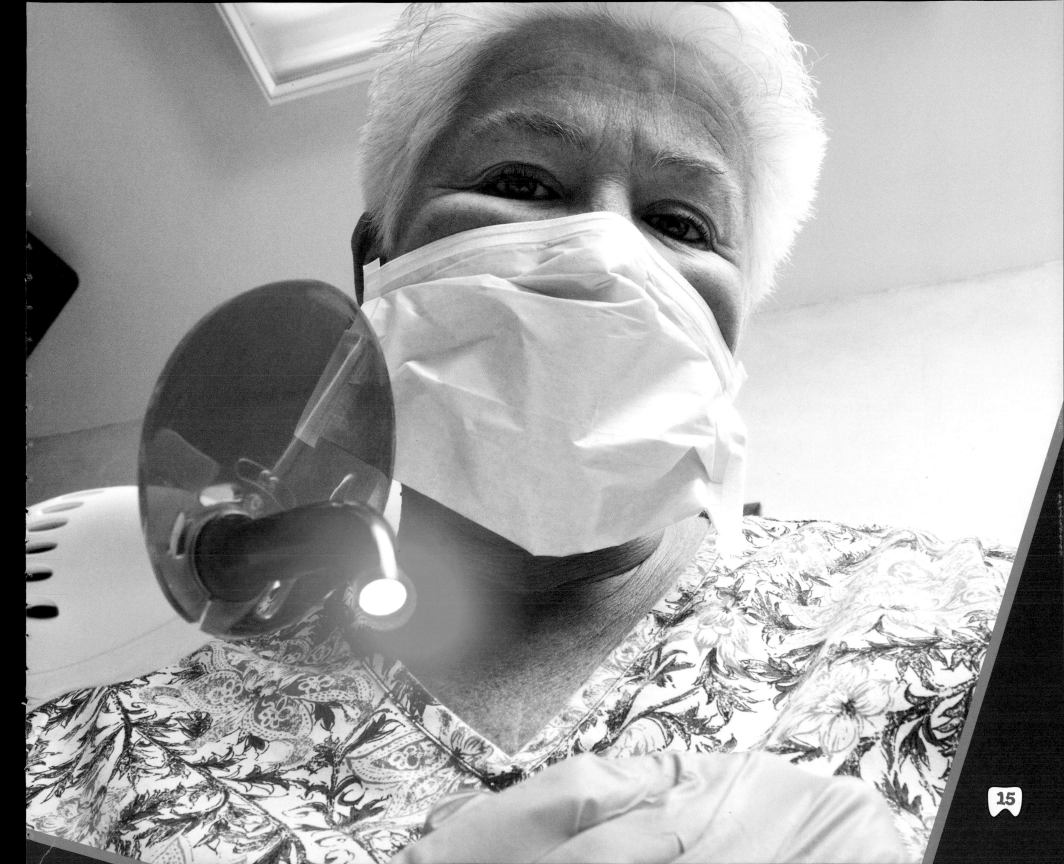

Next, Doug looks
inside Lena's clean mouth
with a small mirror.
He checks for cavities.

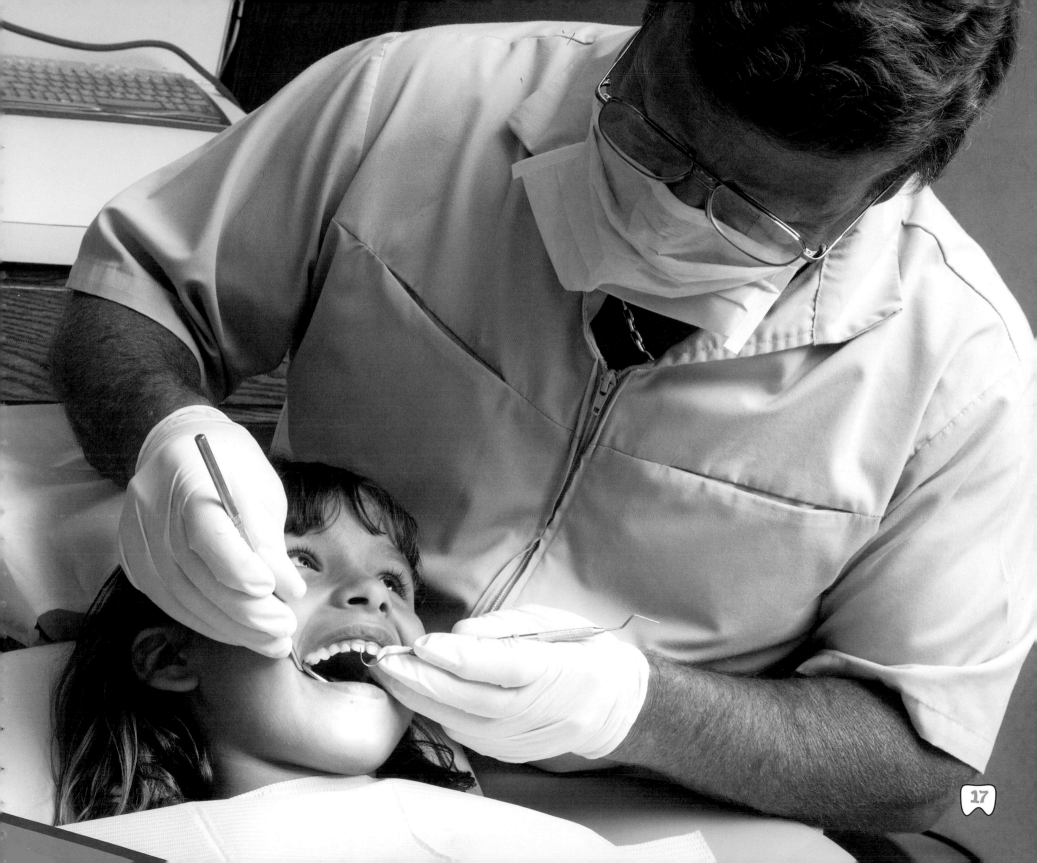

If Lena had a cavity,

Doug would fill it.

But Lena doesn't

have any cavities.

She's all done.

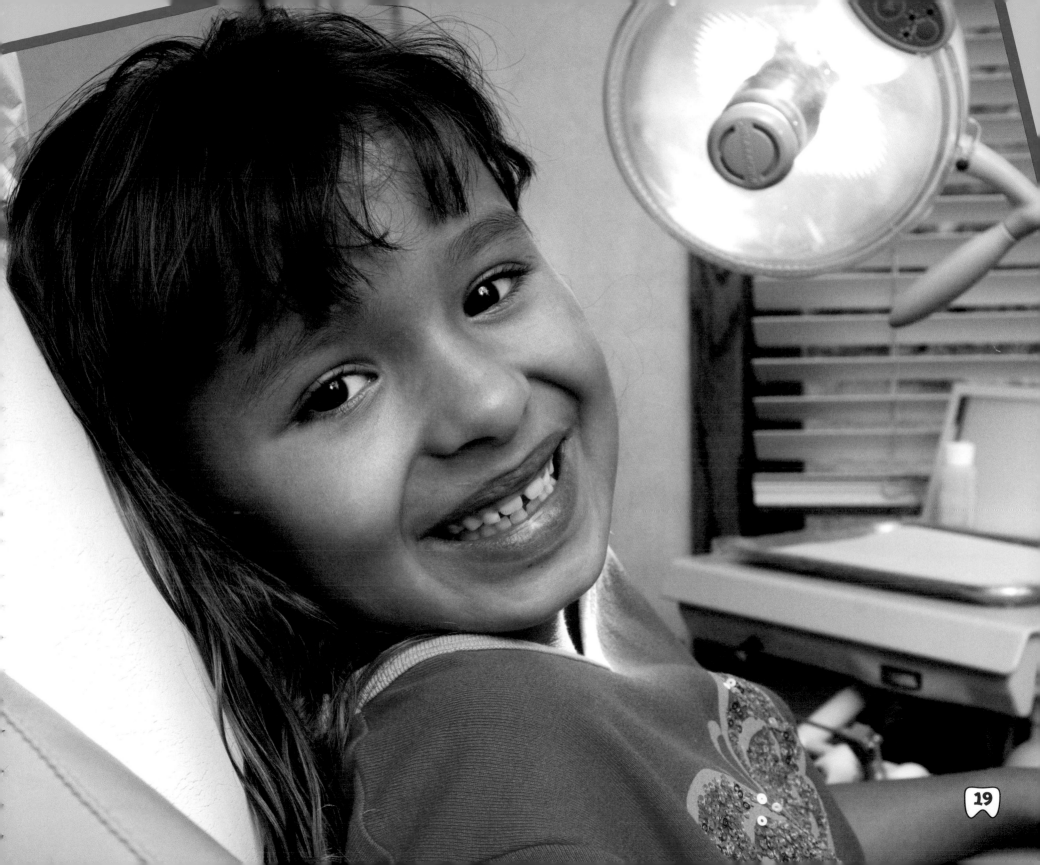

Healthy Teeth

Between dental visits,
Lena brushes and flosses
every day.
She will have a clean,
healthy smile.

Glossary

cavity — a decayed part or hole in a tooth

floss — to put a thin piece of dental floss between your teeth to help keep your teeth clean

hygienist — a person who is trained to clean, polish, and floss teeth; hygienists also take x-rays of teeth and apply flouride and sealants.

plaque — a sticky coating that forms on your teeth from food, bacteria, and saliva in your mouth; plaque causes tooth decay.

polish — to rub something to make it shine

sealant — a plastic coating put on your teeth to help prevent cavities

Read More

Hughes, Monica. *First Visit to the Dentist.* Raintree Sprouts. Chicago: Raintree, 2004.

Minden, Cecilia. *Dentists.* Neighborhood Helpers. Chanhassen, Minn.: Child's World, 2006.

Murphy, Patricia J. *A Visit to the Dentist's Office.* A Visit to. Mankato, Minn.: Capstone Press, 2005.

Internet Sites

FactHound offers a safe, fun way to find Internet sites related to this book. All of the sites on FactHound have been researched by our staff.

Here's how:

1. Visit *www.facthound.com*

2. Choose your grade level.

3. Type in this book ID **1429612428** for age-appropriate sites. You may also browse subjects by clicking on letters, or by clicking on pictures and words.

4. Click on the **Fetch It** button.

FactHound will fetch the best sites for you!

Index

Word Count: 128
Grade: 1
Early-Intervention Level: 18